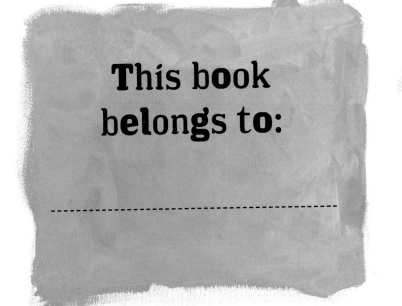

This book belongs to:

For Joe, whose idea it was, and for
Kirsti, whose idea Joe was – C.F.

To Pedja – K.W-M.

Scholastic Children's Books
Commonwealth House, 1-19 New Oxford Street
London WC1A 1NU, UK
a division of Scholastic Ltd
London ~ New York ~ Toronto ~ Sydney ~ Auckland
Mexico City ~ New Delhi ~ Hong Kong

First published in hardback in the UK by Scholastic Ltd, 2005
First published in paperback in the UK by Scholastic Ltd, 2005

Text copyright © Colin Fancy, 2005
Illustrations copyright © Ken Wilson-Max, 2005

ISBN 0 439 95991 8

All rights reserved

Printed in Singapore

2 4 6 8 10 9 7 5 3 1

The rights of Colin Fancy and Ken Wilson-Max to be identified as the author and illustrator
respectively of this work have been asserted by them in accordance with the
Copyright, Designs and Patents Act, 1988.

CROCODILES
Don't Brush Their Teeth

Words by **Colin Fancy**
Pictures by **Ken Wilson-Max**

Hippo

Crocodiles don't brush their teeth.

But I do!

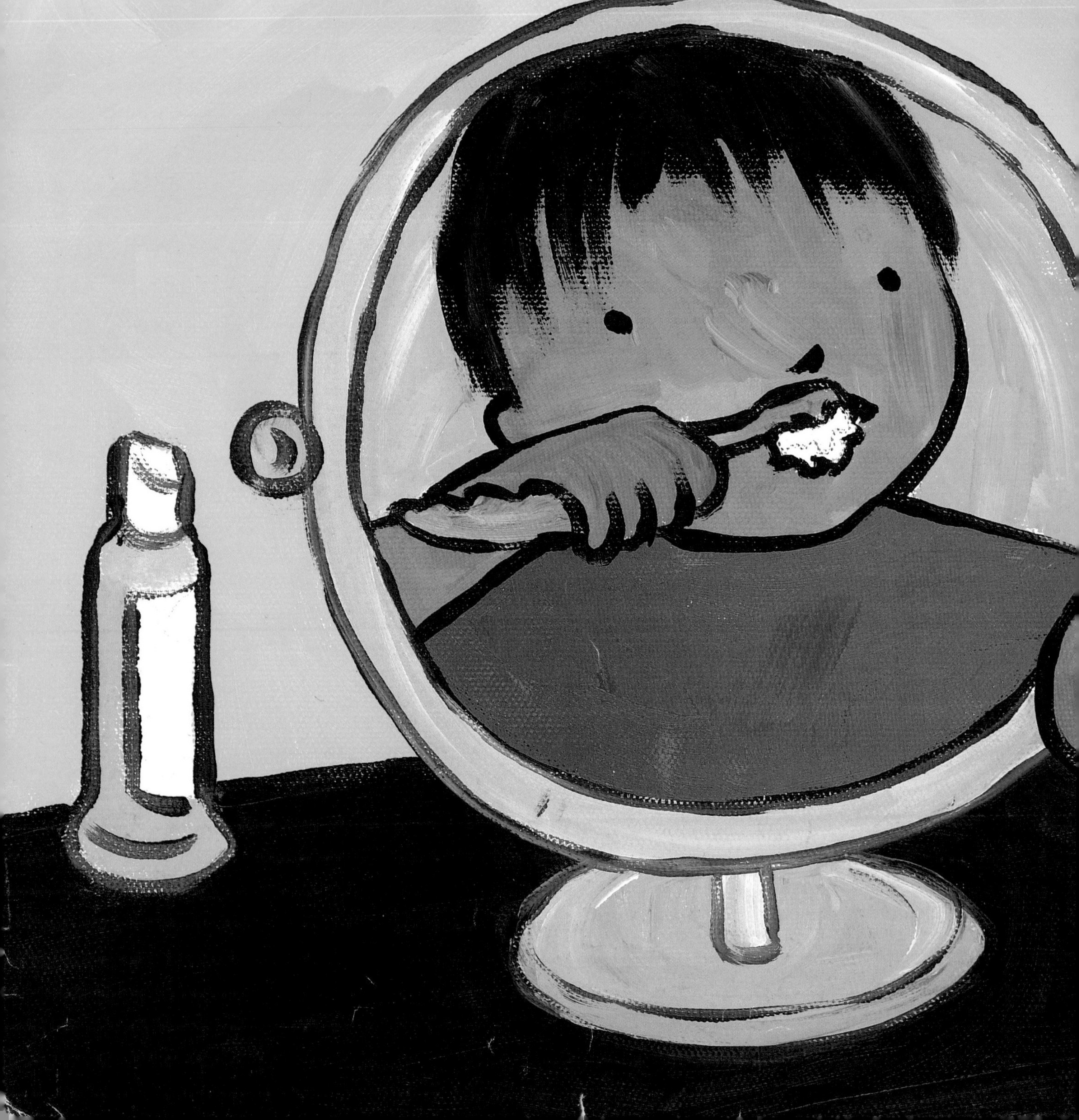

Elephants don't blow their noses.

But I do!

Lions don't brush their hair.

Pigs *don't* wash their faces.

But I do!

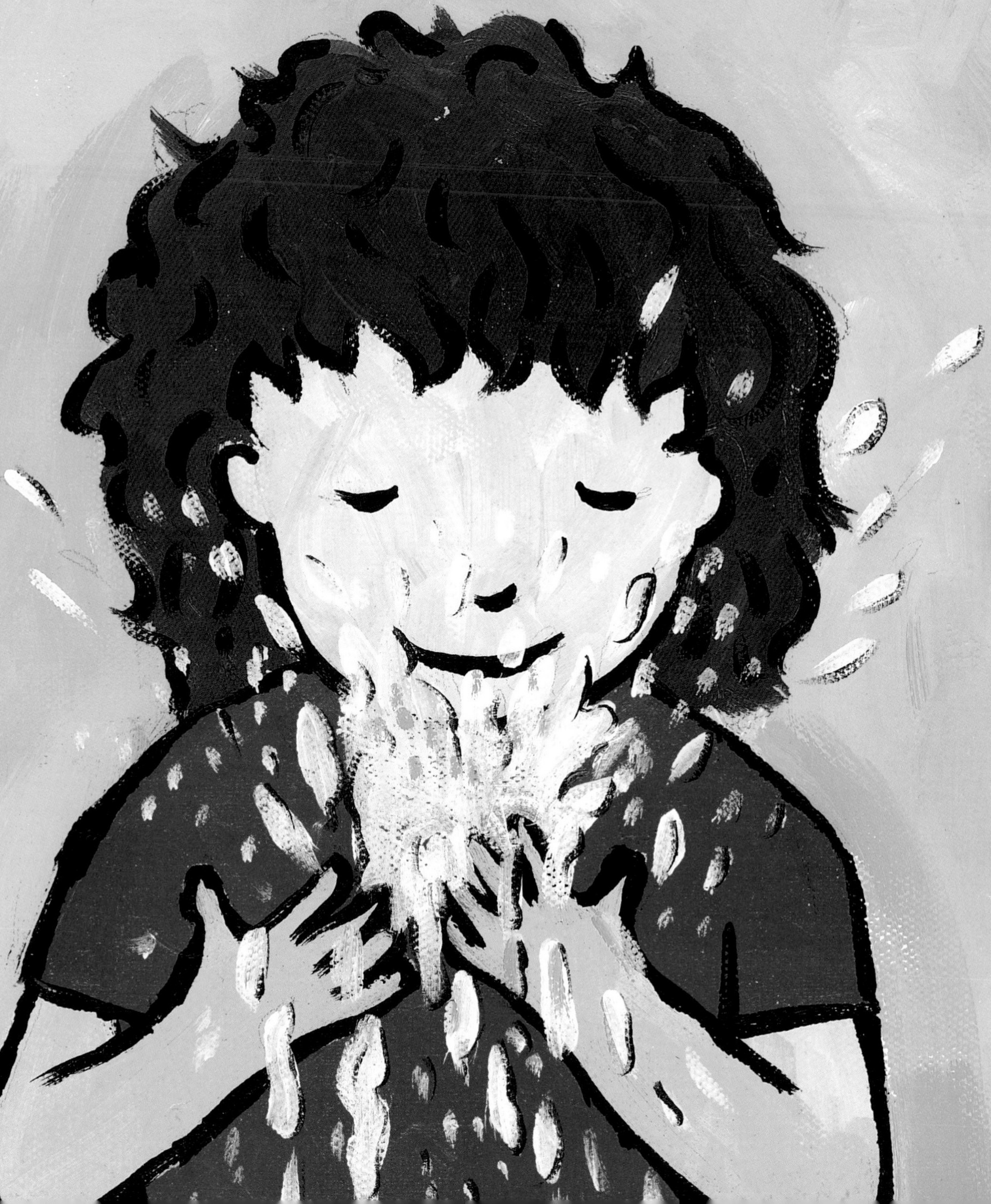

and thank you.

But I do!

Owls
don't *go* to **bed**
at **night**.

But we do!

Do you?